All rights reserved. No part of this publication may be reproduced, stored in a retrieval system, or transmitted in any form or by any means—electronic, mechanical, photocopying, recording, or otherwise—without the prior written permission of the author, except in the case of brief quotations embodied in critical articles or reviews.

Published by:
Be Soulful Coaching
www.bonniestrati.com

Cover Design: Created in collaboration with ChatGPT
Interior Design & Formatting: by the author
Printed in USA

First Edition
ISBN: 979-8-9991515-0-6

This book is a work of nonfiction based on the author's personal experiences and insights. The author has made every effort to ensure the accuracy of the information herein, but this book is not a substitute for professional medical, psychological, or legal advice.

For permissions, bulk orders, speaking engagements, or coaching inquiries, please contact:
✉ bonnie@bonniestrati.com

# Foreword:

# Built Stronger is a Sacred Portal of Inner Alchemy

---

I have walked beside Bonnie Strati for years—not just as her soul guide, but as a witness to her becoming. And what I've seen is not simply the writing of a book, but the living of a sacred initiation.

Built Stronger is not an instruction manual. It is not a self-help book. It is a gateway—a sacred invitation to come home to yourself.

I watched Bonnie, quick with vision and execution, begin to soften. I watched the tender unraveling of who she thought she had to be. I saw the grief, the letting go, the sacred pause. I saw her walk through the liminal dark with her palms open—not knowing where she was going, but choosing, again and again, to trust that the divine would meet her.

This book was forged not in the fire of ambition, but in the slow burn of surrender. And that is why it holds such power.

There are truths in here—not the kind you read, but the kind you become. The kind that lives in the cells of the essence of your being. The kind your sacred ancestors knew. The kind your higher self is still whispering and vibrating through you. It's no surprise that the word, Truth, runs through these pages, because that's what this book is built from - innate universal wisdom.

Other words, too, vibrate through the transmission of this text:

Life. Because this is not theory. It's lived, raw, and real.

Let. Because the medicine here comes through permission - not instruction. Let go. Let in. Let yourself feel.

Even. Because grace lives in the middle of the mess. Even when it hurts. Even in the pause. Even now.

Something. Because this book doesn't try to control what's next. It trusts the emergence. The quiet becoming.

Built Stronger offers no ladder to climb. It offers a spiral. A descent. A softening. And finally, an emergence—not as someone new, but as someone whole.

As a transformational soul guide, I see clearly what Bonnie has done here. She has alchemized. She has taken the sacred raw material of grief, of transition, of stillness—and she has turned it into gold. She has honored the rhythms of the feminine, the intelligence of the nervous system, and the wildness of the soul.

This is not a self-help book. It is a book of self-remembrance.

You may begin reading at any page. You may cry or pause or write or close your eyes. That, too, is part of the medicine.

Let it enter you slowly. Let it speak to the parts of you that have been waiting to be met.

This book is alchemy. A womb. A portal. A return.

And Bonnie? She is no longer rushing toward a future. She is right here. Grounded. Present. Whole.

And, so are you.

— Vanessa Benlolo

Transformational Soul Guide

www.vanessabenlolo.com

# Dedication

To every soul who has walked through fire and emerged softer, stronger, and more whole—
This book is for you.

To my mom, Bea, and my dad, Bob—
Thank you for giving me the space to grow, explore, and evolve without judgment. Your quiet faith in me created the foundation for this journey, and your love continues to hold me in ways words never could.

To my boys, Matt and Nick—
You are two of my greatest teachers. Your lives have shown me the power of love, the lessons of letting go, and the beauty of watching someone you love become who they're meant to be. Thank you for the mirror, the lessons, and the growth.

To my brothers—Bobby, Barry, and Bradley—
You've been my steady ground, my roots in the storm. Your strength and presence have anchored me more times than I can count. I am endlessly grateful for the bond we share.

To my beautiful Aunt Tre—
Your constant support and encouragement have carried me through so many seasons of change. Thank you for believing in me, especially when I was learning to believe in myself.

To my clients—
You inspire me every single day. Thank you for allowing me to walk beside you on your path. Your courage, your breakthroughs, and your willingness to heal are what fuel this work and remind me of the magic in every transformation.

And to you, dear reader—
May these pages meet you wherever you are and walk with you toward wherever you're going. You are not alone. You are not broken. You are beautifully becoming.

With love always,
Bonnie

# Prologue

This book began as a quiet nudge in my heart—a whisper that grew into a truth I could no longer ignore. Through tear-stained journal pages, belly laughs, late-night reflections, and raw conversations, I found myself not just writing, but remembering. At first, I didn't even know I was writing a book. I was simply writing to breathe. To heal. To make sense of it all.

Then something beautiful happened: people began to reach out. "That's exactly how I feel," they'd say. Or, "Thank you. I needed to hear that today." I realized I was not alone in my heartbreak, healing, or becoming. And neither are you.

This book is a collection of truths. It doesn't come from the mountaintop but from the middle of the climb. These stories are about finding strength in the mess, in the pause, and in the decision to keep going—especially when it would be easier to give up.

If you've ever felt stuck, lost, heartbroken, burned out, afraid, or like the universe hit fast-forward on your life without warning—this is for you.

Thank you for holding space for my words. My hope is that they reflect a part of your own journey. May they remind you:

**You're not broken—you're becoming**
With love and deep gratitude,
**Bonnie**

# Introduction

If this book found its way into your hands, trust that it did for a reason.
Maybe you're in a transition.
Maybe you feel the ache of something unfinished.
Maybe you're just longing for a deeper connection—with yourself, your purpose, or the world around you.

This isn't a step-by-step plan. It's a shared space. A series of reflections written during real-life transformation. Each chapter offers insight, grace, and moments of clarity from my journey—and perhaps from yours, too.

You don't have to read this book cover to cover.
Let your intuition guide you. Start where you feel called. Come back to the chapters that speak to your soul.
This is not a book to race through. It's one to journey with.

To support that journey, I created The Built Stronger Journal: A Soulful Companion to Your Transformation—a guided space to help you deepen your reflections, track your emotional shifts, and integrate your growth in real time. Whether you're writing through grief, joy, clarity, or confusion, the journal is a sacred container for your process. Use it alongside this book, or return to it when your heart needs grounding.

However you arrived here, I'm grateful you did.
Let's begin.

With heart,
Bonnie

# Table of Contents

## Part I: Seasons of Life & Letting Go

Chapter 1: The Wake-Up Call ..... 01

Chapter 2: Starting Over Sucks (Until It Doesn't) ..... 07

Chapter 3: Truth Be Told: Freedom Awaits ..... 12

Chapter 4: Thank the Catalysts ..... 17

Chapter 5: When the Universe Hits Fast-Forward on Your Life ..... 22

Chapter 6: Gratitude for Life's Storms and Sunny Skies ..... 27

Chapter 7: Slowing Down: Embracing the Pause Without Panic ..... 32

Chapter 8: The Pain of No Goodbye: Finding Closure Within ..... 37

## Part II: Healing, Truth & Transformation

Chapter 9: Betrayal, Lies, and the Beautiful Mess of Healing ..... 43

Chapter 10: Perfection vs. Reality: Embracing the Mess Leads to True Happiness ..... 49

Chapter 11: Say Goodbye to Self-Doubt: Overcoming Imposter Syndrome and Embracing Your True Power ..... 54

Chapter 12: Reason, Season, Lifetime: Knowing When to Let Go and When to Hold On ..... 59

Chapter 13: The Comfort in Discomfort: Why We Stay Too Long ..... 65

## Part III: Embodiment & Empowerment

Chapter 14: How Vulnerability Unlocks Emotional Strength and Connections ..... 71

Chapter 15: Crossing the Threshold: Where Fear Meets Growth .......................... 76

Chapter 16: Vulnerability as a Superpower: The Gateway to True Connection .......................... 81

Chapter 17: Into the Mystery: Finding Freedom in Letting Go .......................... 86

Chapter 18: The Voice Within: How to Reconnect with Your Inner Wisdom .......................... 92

Chapter 19: Redefining Success: What It Really Means to Win at Life .......................... 97

Chapter 20: Integration: Embodying Your Evolution .................... 103

**Epilogue: The Journey Continues**

# PART 1

## SEASONS OF LIFE & LETTING GO

I trust the pause. I am not lost — I am becoming. Even in stillness, I am being shaped by something sacred.

# Chapter 1:
# The Wake-Up Call

*"We must be willing to let go of the life we have planned, so as to have the life that is waiting for us."*
**– Joseph Campbell**

There are moments in life when everything slows down—not in a peaceful, meditative way, but in a confusing, unsettling way. Like you've found yourself in a waiting room with no name on the door, stuck between who you were and who you're supposed to be. Nothing is falling apart, yet nothing feels quite right. You're doing all the things—working, showing up, moving forward—but a part of you feels frozen in place.

I know this place well. I've lived in it. I've taught classes, answered emails, coached clients, and smiled through social events all while feeling like I was standing still on the inside. Stuck. Searching. Quietly panicking inside a perfectly normal-looking life.

This in-between space is what I call limbo. It's where life puts us when we're ready to grow, but not quite ready to leap. It's the holding ground between comfort and courage. And while it feels like nothing is happening, everything is actually happening.

# Living in Limbo

Limbo is uncomfortable. It stirs up frustration, fear, anxiety, and the need to control. You question your decisions, your relationships, even your purpose. You wonder, "Is something wrong with me?" because everyone else seems to be moving forward while you're… buffering.

But limbo isn't a punishment. It's preparation. It's where clarity brews slowly. Where your spirit has space to speak. Where what's next is being formed beneath the surface.

In one of my own seasons of limbo, I lost a job I had poured my heart into. I thought I'd be relieved—I'd been craving more alignment, more freedom. But when freedom came, I panicked. I felt like I had been unplugged, not just from work, but from identity, structure, and momentum. For the first time in years, I had time. And instead of peace, I felt fear.

I remember one afternoon, sitting on the edge of my bed, staring at a pile of laundry I had no energy to fold. I wasn't tired, just… directionless. The silence in the house was deafening, like life had pressed pause and forgotten to hit play again.

We live in a world that glorifies hustle and productivity. So when life hands us stillness, we don't know what to do with it. We fill it. We numb it. We resist it. But what if slowing down is the very thing that brings us back to life?

Limbo feels like walking through fog—you can't see what's ahead, but you know the path is still there. It's like living inside parentheses, waiting for the sentence of your life to start again.

## A Season for Everything

Looking back, I realized that my life had always moved in seasons. I had a five-year season as a competitive bodybuilder. Then a five-year season devoted to yoga. Later, tennis. And each time a season began to fade, I fought it—afraid to lose that part of me, afraid of who I'd be without it.

But life doesn't ask us to stay the same. It invites us to evolve. To release what's complete and embrace what's next. Sometimes gracefully, sometimes kicking and screaming. And when we resist those changes, we burn out.

There's no shame in outgrowing things. Activities. Jobs. Even people. Some are meant to be reasons. Some seasons. And a few lifetimes. Learning which is which is part of our growth.

We fear the unknown, so we cling to what we've known—even if it no longer fits. The familiar, even when it's limiting, feels safer than the possibility of expansion. But true transformation requires release. It asks us to loosen our grip.

And here's the thing—there is beauty in becoming. In the quiet dismantling of the old, and the slow, sacred construction of something new. You are not behind. You are unfolding.

Nature never rushes. Spring doesn't arrive before winter completes its purpose. There is sacredness in the stillness. There is growth even in dormancy.

## Finding Meaning in the Pause

What if your current stuckness is not a stop sign, but a sacred pause? What if this is your soul's way of rerouting you toward something more aligned?

Limbo isn't forever. But it is fertile ground. It's where dreams get reimagined. Where healing begins. Where new desires are born.

Instead of rushing out of it, what if you asked:

- What is this stillness showing me?
- What part of me is asking to be heard?
- What is no longer sustainable in my life?

These aren't easy questions. But they are the kind that lead to transformation. To living from the inside out.

Here's something I've witnessed in my coaching work—a woman in her mid-50s who had spent decades climbing the corporate ladder, always in control, always the one others leaned on. Then one day, her carefully constructed life began to unravel—not with one dramatic event, but through a series of subtle shifts. Her grown children needed her less. Her work no longer lit her up. Her body was sending signals she couldn't ignore.

At first, she tried to power through—more plans, more productivity, more pushing. But the more she tried to grip control, the more exhausted she became. Eventually, she came to our sessions not for strategy, but for stillness. Slowly, she started to listen—not to the world, but to herself.

She began to rest, to breathe, to reconnect with the passions she had buried beneath obligation. And in doing so, she didn't fall apart—she came home to herself. She left the title behind and started mentoring women on their own midlife journeys. Her life got quieter, but so much fuller. And most of all, it got honest.

Her story is a reminder: the pause is powerful.

## Soul Check-In Practice

Find a quiet space. Place your hands over your heart and ask, "What truth have I been too busy to hear?"

Breathe. Write down what comes. Let it be messy. Don't judge it. This is not about answers—it's about allowing truth to rise.

And if you feel overwhelmed by the stillness, try this grounding moment:

**Grounding Practice:** Take three deep breaths. Place one hand on your belly and the other on your chest. Feel the rise and fall. You are not broken—you are becoming.

What I didn't know then was that letting go wasn't the end—it was the initiation. The truth was, the version of me I was clinging to had already outgrown her container. And as I began to loosen my grip, something unexpected started to bloom.

A quieter self. A wiser self. One not driven by proving, performing, or producing—but by presence, peace, and possibility.

So if you're here—in the fog, the in-between, the pause—take heart. You're not lost. You're landing. And what's next is not waiting "out there." It's unfolding inside of you, one breath, one step, one brave yes at a time.

You are not falling apart—you are falling into place.

# Chapter 2:

# Starting Over Sucks (Until It Doesn't)

*"And suddenly you just know... it's time to start something new and trust the magic of beginnings."*
— **Meister Eckhart**

No one wakes up and says, "Today I want to start my life over." Most of us cling tightly to what we know—even when what we know is exhausting, unfulfilling, or no longer aligned. But life? Life has a way of deciding for us.

Sometimes the beginning of something new shows up disguised as the ending of something familiar. A job loss. A breakup. A breakdown. A diagnosis. A pandemic. A plot twist you didn't see coming. It sneaks up like a storm—you don't realize you're in the middle of it until everything around you looks different.

When it happened to me, I didn't feel hopeful. I felt broken. Starting over wasn't exciting—it was terrifying. I wanted clarity and I got chaos. I wanted confidence and I got fear. I wanted answers and I got silence. But here's the truth: starting over always sucks at first. Until it doesn't.

## The Grief of Letting Go

Before we begin something new, we have to mourn what was. And that grief isn't always about losing something great—it's often about losing something known. Certainty. Routine. Identity. The comfort of expectations, even if those expectations were slowly suffocating us.

I had to grieve the version of my life I thought I wanted. The role I had built around myself. The relationships I thought were forever. The version of me who had it all figured out. And it was messy. Crying-into-my-pillow kind of messy. Journaling-until-my-hand-ached kind of messy. But grief has a sacred place in growth. It clears the space for something truer.

Sometimes grief doesn't come with big, dramatic tears. Sometimes it's numbness. A strange quiet. A constant question: "Now what?" You might not realize you're grieving until you catch yourself missing even the parts you didn't love. That's okay. That's human.

It's also important to note that grief doesn't follow a straight line. You might feel strong one day and undone the next. You might find moments of laughter tucked into days of sadness. That's not regression—it's release. It's your heart making room.

## The Possibility in the Unknown

Once the tears dry—or even while they're still falling—something surprising starts to happen. You begin to notice a spark—tiny, flickering hope. You have space to dream again. You're not who you were, and you're not quite who you're becoming, but you're on your way.

In the stillness, I began to ask better questions:

- What lights me up?
- What am I no longer willing to tolerate?
- If I weren't afraid, what would I do?

These questions didn't give me a five-year plan. But they gave me a starting point. And sometimes, that's all you need. A breadcrumb. A whisper. A direction, not a destination.

I remember one afternoon, sitting in my car with a green juice in one hand and a tear-stained napkin in the other. I had just left a yoga class that cracked me open, not because of the postures, but because the teacher said something that landed in my chest like a truth bomb: "The way you begin again is by standing still long enough to hear what your soul is saying."

I sat in that car for what felt like forever. And I heard it—my own voice, faint but steady, whispering, "There's more for you than this."

That day marked the beginning of a shift—not externally, but internally. It was the first time I started to trust the flickers of something new, even though I didn't have the full picture yet. It was enough to begin. And that was everything.

## The Courage to Redefine

Starting over gives you the rare opportunity to ask, "Who am I now?" Not who you used to be. Not who others expect you to be. But who you want to be moving forward.

I began to rebuild. Slowly. Imperfectly. I created new routines. I reached out to mentors. I changed what I consumed—books, food, energy. I let go of what didn't fit anymore. And with each brave choice, I came home to myself.

I learned that courage isn't about having it all figured out. It's about showing up anyway. It's about taking the next step with a shaky voice and a hopeful heart. It's about trusting that you are not behind—you are becoming.

The best part? I didn't have to become someone new. I just had to remember who I was underneath it all. The parts of me that had been buried under expectations, survival mode, and stories that were never really mine.

## Your New Beginning

If you're at the edge of a fresh start, know this: You're not starting from scratch. You're starting from experience, strength, and wisdom. From everything you've already overcome. From every moment you thought you wouldn't survive, but did.

You've already survived what you feared. You've already proven you can get back up. So now, the question becomes: what do you want to build?

Here's a gentle practice for your heart:

## New Beginning Ritual

Take out a journal and write a letter—not to who you were, but to who you're becoming. Thank your past self for your strength, and let your future self know: I'm on my way.

And if you want to go deeper: create a vision board or write out a list of the values you want to live by in this next season. Not goals—values. Things like: integrity, spaciousness, joy, curiosity, truth. Let these become your compass.

This is your blank page. Write something bold. Write something honest. Write something just for you. Because even if starting over sucks at first, it's also how we find magic again.

And trust me, that magic? It's waiting.

## Affirmation for the Journey:

"I honor the endings I didn't choose, the new paths I didn't expect, and the strength that kept me going. I am not starting over. I am starting ahead—with wisdom in my bones and hope in my heart."

# Chapter 3:
# Truth Be Told – Freedom Awaits

*"The truth will set you free, but first it will piss you off."*
— **Gloria Steinem**

We say we want the truth. But let's be honest—truth is not always neat. It doesn't show up with a welcome mat and a scented candle. It often arrives like a lightning bolt, slicing through the illusions we've worked so hard to maintain. It doesn't always feel like a gift. It can feel like a gut punch. A betrayal. A collapse. But in hindsight? Truth is always liberation in disguise.

For a long time, I lived with half-truths. I told myself I was fine. That I could keep making everything work. That I didn't need to rock the boat. That being loyal to other people's comfort was more important than being honest with myself. But there came a moment when the weight of all that pretending became too much. The cost of staying silent, of staying small, was no longer bearable. And that's when truth came crashing in—loud, messy, and completely uninvited.

# When Truth Whispers—and Then Roars

Truth doesn't always arrive as a revelation. Sometimes it starts as a whisper. A quiet knowing. A gut feeling. An inner nudge that something is off. You try to ignore it. You push it down. You distract yourself with busyness or blame. But truth is persistent. If ignored long enough, it roars. It will find a way to get your attention.

I remember sitting across from someone I deeply cared about, listening to their words while my body screamed, "This isn't it." On the surface, everything seemed okay. But underneath, I could feel the disconnect. The dishonesty. The misalignment. And I had to face the most uncomfortable question: What truth am I avoiding?

The Lies We Tell Ourselves

We all do it. We tell ourselves things to avoid pain:

- "They didn't mean it."
- "This is just a rough patch."
- "Maybe it's my fault."
- "I'm asking for too much."

But deep down, we know when something is off. We know when we're shrinking, twisting, or betraying ourselves to maintain a sense of peace that isn't real. The problem with these lies is that they pile up. And eventually, they collapse.

Owning our truth means calling ourselves out—not in shame, but in liberation. It means saying: "This version of my life no longer fits."

## Truth as a Doorway

Truth is not a wrecking ball. It's a doorway. Yes, it may knock down what's no longer meant for you. But it also opens you to what is. It creates space for clarity, alignment, and new possibilities. It allows you to breathe again. To show up fully. To live in integrity with your heart.

In my own experience, once I finally spoke the truth I had been avoiding, something shifted. Yes, it was scary. Yes, I faced resistance and fear and grief. But I also felt lighter. More alive. More myself. The weight I'd been carrying wasn't from the situation—it was from hiding the truth.

## The Truth About Others

Sometimes, the hardest truth to accept is that someone isn't who we hoped they'd be. That they aren't capable of the love, presence, or honesty we need. And that's not a judgment—it's a clarity.

We can love someone and still acknowledge they're not meant to stay. We can wish them well and still walk away. Truth doesn't always require conflict. Sometimes, it simply requires acceptance.

If you're waiting for someone to change, ask yourself: Are you loving them as they are, or are you loving their potential? Because loving someone's potential is often a way of abandoning your present needs.

## The Practice of Living Truth

Telling the truth isn't a one-time event. It's a daily practice. It's in how you speak, how you choose, and how you show up for yourself. And it's okay if it's hard. It's okay if you tremble when you say it. Courage doesn't mean you're not afraid—it means you speak anyway.

**Truth-Telling Journal Prompt:** Write down three truths you've been avoiding. Start each one with, "The truth is…" Then pause. Breathe. Let them exist without needing to fix anything.

**Self-Honoring Mantra:** "I am safe to see clearly. I honor my truth, even when it's uncomfortable. I release what no longer aligns so I can step into what does."

## The Freedom on the Other Side

Truth is not always easy—but it's always worth it. On the other side of honesty is freedom. Freedom to be yourself. Freedom to breathe deeply. Freedom to build a life that actually reflects your values and desires.

So if you're feeling the nudge—if your inner voice is getting louder—trust it. Truth is not here to ruin your life. It's here to return you to it.

And once you start living in truth, you'll never want to go back to pretending again.

**Affirmation to Anchor This Chapter:** "I trust the wisdom of my truth. It may shake things up, but it always leads me home."

# Chapter 4:
# Thank the Catalyst

*"Some changes look negative on the surface, but you will soon realize that space is being created in your life for something new to emerge."*
– Eckhart Tolle

Life doesn't always offer gentle nudges. Sometimes it shows up like a bulldozer. The kind that flattens your carefully curated plans and routines and leaves you standing in the rubble, wide-eyed and wondering what the hell just happened. It doesn't ask if you're ready. It just moves. It shatters. It rearranges. And only later, if you're lucky, does it reveal the purpose behind the chaos.

## When Life Turns Upside Down

Maybe it was a job loss. A health scare. A relationship ending that you didn't see coming. A betrayal that knocked the wind out of you. These moments are jarring. They make you feel like the ground beneath you is shifting, and you're grasping for something—anything—to hold onto.

I've had my world turned upside down more than once. It never felt good. It felt cruel. It felt like the universe had forgotten I was trying my best. But now, looking back, those were the exact moments that cracked me open. That demanded I wake up. That forced me to stop pretending everything was fine and start asking what was actually true.

Because here's the thing: disruption is often divine. It doesn't feel like it when you're crying on the kitchen floor or staring blankly at the ceiling at 3 a.m. But that unraveling? That discomfort? It's a sacred invitation to realign.

Sometimes it doesn't just feel like you're losing something—it feels like you're losing everything. And in a way, you are. You're losing the illusion that you were in control. You're losing the version of yourself that settled for less. And yes, that loss hurts. But it also creates space—big, beautiful, open space—for something far more aligned to emerge.

## The Role of the Catalyst

Catalysts come in many forms—people, events, illnesses, betrayals, losses. And while we rarely welcome them, they arrive with purpose. They push us to grow. They shine light on the parts of our lives that are out of sync with our soul. They challenge the roles we've been playing and the stories we've been telling.

I used to get angry at the people who hurt me. I wanted apologies, closure, understanding. But with time, I realized they were never meant to stay. They were meant to trigger something in me that needed healing. They were mirrors, showing me where I was still betraying myself. Where I was shrinking. Where I was settling.

The partner who couldn't show up? He taught me I needed to show up for myself. The job that burned me out? It taught me I was allowed to choose peace over proving. The friend who ghosted me? She reminded me that not everyone is meant for the whole ride.

And I've learned this too: Sometimes you are the catalyst in someone else's story. Sometimes your growth, your boundary, your decision to walk away, is the thing that jolts another person out of their comfort zone. And while that may feel heavy, it's also holy.

## Gratitude in the Mess

It sounds wild, I know. Being grateful for the mess? For the pain? For the ones who hurt you? But gratitude doesn't mean you're glad it happened. It means you're willing to harvest the wisdom from it. It means you're no longer letting the wound define you—you're letting it shape you.

Try this: **Catalyst Reflection Practice:** Think back to a painful ending in your life. Write it out—what happened, how it felt, what you lost. Then write about what it made room for. What came after? What did you learn about yourself? How did you rise?

This practice isn't about bypassing the pain. It's about reclaiming your power.

We get to choose how we integrate the experiences that shattered us. We can either stay broken or we can gather the pieces and build something more true, more bold, more us.

## What the Catalysts Taught Me

Every catalyst in my life has peeled back another layer of who I thought I had to be. They dismantled the walls I built around my heart. They broke the illusion of control. And in their wake, they left something precious: truth. Alignment. Freedom.

Here's what I've learned:

- You don't have to love the catalyst. You just have to let it teach you.
- Not everyone is meant to stay—and that doesn't mean you failed.
- Growth is rarely comfortable, but it's always worth it.
- Pain can be sacred. Let it be a portal.

When you stop resisting what is, you make space for what can be.

## Your Turn to Reflect

If you're walking through chaos right now, pause and ask:

- What is this season showing me?
- What part of me is being called to evolve?
- Where am I being asked to surrender?
- Can I soften instead of brace?

Remember: Sometimes the breakdown is the breakthrough. And sometimes the breakthrough begins when you simply stop pretending you're okay.

**Affirmation to Anchor This Chapter:** "I bless the people and moments that cracked me open. They didn't break me—they built me. I trust the mess to mold me into someone even more aligned with my truth."

Because you, my love, were never meant to stay small. And sometimes, it takes a catalyst to remind you of that.

And when the dust settles, you'll see—you were always being guided home to yourself.

## Chapter 5:

# When the Universe Hits Fast-Forward on Your Life

*"Sometimes when things are falling apart, they may actually be falling into place."*
— **Unknown**

Life has a funny way of speeding up just when we think we've finally settled into a rhythm. One moment you're cruising along, thinking you've got time to figure things out, and the next—bam—the universe slams a door shut, throws open a window, and cranks your life into high gear. It's disorienting. It's uncomfortable. And—if you let it—it's wildly transformative.

## Recognizing the Shift

Sometimes the signs of change are subtle: a low hum of unease, a restlessness that won't quit, an intuitive whisper that something's off. You sense the change before it arrives, but it's easy to brush off. After all, nothing's "wrong" on the surface. So you stay.

Other times, the universe doesn't whisper. It roars. A job ends abruptly. A relationship collapses. Your health demands a reset. Your lease isn't renewed. Suddenly, life doesn't ask you to change—it demands it. And you're standing in the rubble of what was, not quite sure how to begin again.

For me, it came as a series of events that left me no choice but to move. I had been lingering in uncertainty, craving more but hesitating to leap. I thought I had time. I thought I could control the pace. But the universe had other plans. It stepped in and gave me the shove I hadn't dared to take myself. And yes, I was scared. But I was also cracked open in the best way.

Sometimes it feels like everything is shifting all at once—friends fall away, opportunities dissolve, and even your daily rhythm begins to unravel. And while part of you clings to the familiar, another part of you knows: something bigger is unfolding.

## Why the Universe Pushes

When we delay the changes we know deep down we need to make, life often intervenes. Not out of cruelty—but out of love. It's not punishment. It's alignment.

The fast-forward moments come to shake us from our comfort zone. To clear out the clutter. To release the illusions we've clung to. To show us what's possible beyond our perceived limitations.

We won't always walk through the door willingly. So sometimes, the universe slams it shut and tosses us through a window instead. It's messy. It's jarring. But it's also the very thing that gets us moving.

You might not feel ready. But readiness isn't a requirement for growth. Willingness is.

It's in these sudden accelerations that we often find our deepest truths. We're forced to ask questions we've been avoiding. We confront our patterns, our fears, our unfinished healing. And while we may feel like we're being spun around in a cosmic washing machine, what's actually happening is a deep clearing. An energetic reset. A soul realignment.

## Navigating the Acceleration

If you find yourself suddenly thrust into change, here's what helped me stay grounded:

**Pause and Breathe:** Don't rush to fix it. Let yourself feel everything. Shock. Anger. Grief. Hope. Give your nervous system time to catch up with your new reality.

**Flip the Perspective:** Try asking, "How could this be happening for me instead of to me?" This question won't erase the pain, but it opens the door to possibility.

**Look for the Opening:** Instead of only focusing on what ended, gently shift your attention toward what might now be possible. What space just got cleared? What longing was buried beneath the routine?

**Take One Step:** You don't need the entire map. You just need the next right step. The clarity comes in the doing.

**Anchor in Ritual:** In the chaos of transition, create little anchors. Morning tea in silence. Five deep breaths before bed. A walk at the same time each day. Ritual reminds your body and spirit that you are safe in motion.

# Riding the Wave of Change

When life hits fast-forward, your job is not to control every outcome. Your job is to stay present. Stay open. Stay curious. This is a time to trust the momentum, even if you don't understand it yet.

You are not being thrown off track. You're being accelerated onto a different one—one that's likely more in alignment with who you're becoming. Let go of the old timeline. This is your new beginning.

And yes, it may be uncomfortable. You may feel unsteady. But growth often feels like chaos in the beginning. That doesn't mean it's wrong. It means it's real.

These seasons call us to step out of the timeline we thought we were on and into the mystery. To trust the unfolding, even when we don't know where it leads. To remember that we're not starting over—we're starting deeper.

## What Comes Next

In hindsight, I see now that the acceleration was a gift. It shook me awake. It stripped away what I was clinging to so I could reach for something better. It didn't destroy my plans—it upgraded them. It rerouted me toward more purpose, more freedom, more truth.

I thought I needed a map. What I needed was trust.

Here's a soul-nourishing prompt to support you:

**Fast-Forward Reflection Practice:** Write about a time when your life shifted quickly—when something unexpected changed your direction. What did it break open in you? What new opportunities came from it? What version of yourself began to emerge?

And this reminder, which has carried me through many rapid resets:

**Affirmation to Anchor This Chapter:** "Even in the chaos, I am guided. I trust the detours. I welcome the redirections. I am being moved, not lost."

When the universe speeds things up, it's not because you're behind—it's because you're ready. Even if you don't feel like it.

And sometimes, the fast lane is exactly what your soul ordered.

Hold on tight, love. You're on your way.

## Chapter 6:

# Gratitude for Life's Storms and Sunny Skies

---

*"Gratitude is a powerful catalyst for happiness. It's the spark that lights a fire of joy in your soul."*
— **Amy Collette**

Gratitude doesn't always arrive like a gift wrapped in bows and sunshine. Sometimes it crawls in after the storm, drenched and humbled, whispering, "Look at how far you've come."

## The Gift of Hindsight

In the thick of it, pain feels like punishment. The storm clouds gather. The winds of uncertainty howl. And you wonder, "Why is this happening to me?" But with time—and a little grace—that pain transforms into purpose. What once felt like an unbearable storm slowly reveals itself to be the very rain that nurtured your growth.

Gratitude doesn't always show up in real time. Sometimes, it arrives in hindsight, like sunlight breaking through after a long, gray season. It takes root in quiet moments—when you realize the thing that once broke your heart taught you how to keep it open without letting it shatter again. When you see the detour wasn't a distraction, but divine direction.

The loss, the heartbreak, the unexpected detour—each of them left a mark. A scar. A shift. And yet, looking back, I can see how those marks became milestones. They led me to deeper clarity, greater strength, and a kind of joy that only exists on the other side of struggle.

Sometimes we don't know we're healing until we're standing in the sunshine again, breathing deeply, feeling something close to peace. And in those sacred pauses, gratitude blooms.

## Reflection as a Pathway to Gratitude

Reflection is what turns experience into wisdom. When we pause long enough to look back—not just to relive, but to learn—we start to recognize the subtle ways life has been guiding us all along. The closed doors that protected us. The delays that bought us time. The disappointments that rerouted us to something better.

Gratitude blooms in the soil of perspective. The more willing we are to slow down and reflect, the more we begin to see that nothing was wasted. Every twist, every tear, every "not yet" had something to teach us.

Try this gentle inquiry:

## Gratitude Reflection Questions:

- What challenge shaped me the most this past year?
- What did it teach me about myself, about others, about life?
- Where was grace hidden in the chaos?
- What surprised me about my own strength?

These questions hold the keys to discovering gratitude in the very places we once wanted to escape. It doesn't mean we loved the storm—but we honor what it made possible.

## Shifting the Lens

Gratitude isn't about pretending everything's fine. It's not toxic positivity or spiritual bypassing. It's about acknowledging the full spectrum of your experience—the joy and the pain, the wins and the wounds—and choosing to see the value in all of it.

It's saying: "That was hard. That broke me open. And somehow, I'm better for it."

The shift from victimhood to gratitude is subtle but powerful. It's not about denying the hardship; it's about honoring your resilience. It's about claiming your growth and recognizing the sacred wisdom your journey gave you.

And here's the truth most people don't say out loud: sometimes we're grateful not just for what happened, but for what didn't. For the love that never came back. For the job we didn't get. For the friend who left. Because without those no's, we wouldn't have been available for the yeses that changed everything.

## Everyday Gratitude

Gratitude doesn't always need a big revelation. It can live in the tiny, ordinary moments too. The warmth of your morning coffee. A kind text from a friend. The quiet comfort of your breath. These are sacred, too.

If you're feeling stuck in the storm, start there. One small thing. One soft thank you. One breath. And let it grow.

**Gratitude Practice:** Each night before bed, write down three things you're grateful for. They can be simple: the sound of rain, a deep conversation, a moment of laughter. This small ritual rewires your mind to look for goodness—even when life is messy.

And if you can't find gratitude yet, that's okay. It will come. Sometimes just surviving is enough. Sometimes just getting through the day is something to celebrate. Trust that the light always returns.

## What Gratitude Has Shown Me

Gratitude has taught me to meet life with softness instead of resistance. To embrace both the sunny skies and the storms. To hold joy and sorrow in the same breath and know they both belong.

It's shown me that every ending holds a new beginning, that every breakdown has the seeds of a breakthrough, and that sometimes, the most sacred growth is invisible to the world but undeniable to the soul.

So here's what I want you to remember:

You don't have to be grateful for the pain, but you can be grateful for who you became because of it.

And in that way, gratitude becomes your alchemy. It turns wounds into wisdom. It turns chaos into clarity. It turns life—messy, beautiful, unpredictable life—into a sacred unfolding.

Let that be your anchor the next time the storm rolls in.

**Affirmation to Anchor This Chapter:** "I honor my journey—all of it. I find gratitude not just in what was easy, but in what made me strong. I trust that even the storms are shaping me into someone wiser, deeper, and more aligned."

Gratitude is not the end of the story. It's how we begin again, with eyes wide open and hearts fully alive.

# Chapter 7:

# Slowing Down: Embracing the Pause Without Panic

*"Almost everything will work again if you unplug it for a few minutes, including you."*
— **Anne Lamott**

We spend so much of our lives rushing—from one task, one goal, one responsibility to the next. We crave more time, yet when it finally arrives, wrapped in stillness and space, we panic.

I used to dream of having more moments to breathe, to reflect, to finally catch up on everything I said I'd get to "someday." Then, without warning, the universe gave me exactly that. And instead of the peace I envisioned, I was met with anxiety.

No calendar. No deadlines. Just space. And silence.

## The Unexpected Gift of Stillness

We live in a culture that celebrates busyness. Hustle is glorified. Rest is romanticized but rarely respected. So when life slows us down—whether by choice or circumstance—it can feel like we've lost our footing.

But what if the pause isn't the problem? What if it's the invitation?

Stillness can feel disorienting at first, especially when our worth has been tied to productivity. When the outer noise fades, we are left with the inner voices—the ones we've been too busy to hear.

For me, the pause came in the form of lost work. On paper, it looked like freedom. But inside, I felt untethered. My mind screamed: Am I falling behind? What if I never get back on track? Who am I without the to-do list?

And then, slowly, another voice emerged: What if this is exactly what I needed?

## The Fear Behind Stillness

Stillness is often mistaken for stagnation. But more often, it's fertile ground for transformation.

When the busyness stops, all the feelings we've been outrunning come forward. The doubt. The grief. The longing. The dreams we shelved. That's why so many of us resist the quiet—we fear what we'll find in the silence.

But the truth is, the silence is where truth lives.

We can't heal what we won't face. And we can't hear what life is trying to tell us when we're moving too fast to listen.

Stillness isn't empty. It's full of messages—but only if we're willing to receive them.

## Learning to Sit With the Silence

Slowing down isn't about doing nothing. It's about doing things differently. With presence. With care. With attention.

I started small. Mornings without screens. Just breath, maybe a stretch, a few honest lines in my journal. I let walks be walks—not workouts. I watched the trees. I listened to the birds. I let myself notice again.

I traded urgency for curiosity. Perfectionism for presence. Slowly, the panic softened. And I began to listen—to myself, to my body, to what life was asking of me.

It was in that stillness that my clarity returned. Not all at once, but piece by piece.

And you know what else returned? My creativity. My sense of wonder. The spark that had dimmed from overdoing. Turns out, my soul didn't want more effort. It wanted more presence.

## The Reframe: Rest as Progress

Rest isn't lazy. It's sacred. It's a vital part of the cycle of growth.

We don't demand that seeds bloom every day. We trust their timing. We honor the dark soil where roots are forming. Why don't we offer ourselves the same grace?

Some of the most transformative moments in my life came not through hustle, but through surrender. Through the quiet mornings. The long walks. The tears I finally let fall. That's when clarity arrived. That's when I remembered who I was beneath the striving.

Instead of asking, "What should I be doing?" I started asking, "What is this moment asking of me?"

That shift changed everything.

# What Slowing Down Taught Me

**Presence is Powerful** – Life is happening now. Not someday. Not when you have it all figured out. Now.

**Rest Fuels Growth** – Burnout doesn't make you better. Rest does. Integration matters just as much as action.

**Stillness Holds Answers** – When the noise quiets, your inner knowing grows louder.

**Peace Is an Inside Job** – And it starts with permission. Permission to slow down, to feel, to listen, to just be.

Here's a simple practice that helped me reconnect:

**Sacred Pause Practice:** Each day, take five minutes to sit quietly. No distractions. Just breathe. Notice what arises without judgment. Write down one thing your soul whispers. Over time, these whispers become your compass.

## Final Thoughts

If you find yourself in a forced pause—whether by choice or by circumstance—know this: it's not a setback. It's a recalibration. A sacred reset. A moment between chapters.

Let the quiet shape you. Let it soften you. Let it guide you.

Because sometimes, when we stop running, we finally see where we are. And from that place of presence, the next chapter can begin—not in panic, but in peace.

You are not lost. You are landing.

**Affirmation to Anchor This Chapter:** "I am allowed to slow down. I trust the stillness. I honor the sacred pause as part of my becoming."

This isn't the end, love. It's the beginning of something quieter, wiser, and deeply aligned.

# Chapter 8:

# The Pain of No Goodbye: Finding Closure Within

*"When someone shows you who they are, believe them the first time."*
**— Maya Angelou**

There are few heartbreaks more painful than being left without a goodbye. Whether it's a relationship that faded into silence, a friendship that vanished without explanation, or a loved one taken too soon, the ache of unfinished endings lingers. It's an ache that settles in the chest like a weight. We crave resolution. We want the final words, the chance to understand, to make sense of what just happened.

But sometimes, closure doesn't come from others. It comes from within. And while that truth may sting, it's also incredibly empowering. Learning to give ourselves the grace and closure we never received from someone else can be the most healing, soul-affirming act we ever do.

# The Ache of Unfinished Endings

Goodbyes help us process. They mark a transition. They create a boundary between what was and what is. When we're denied that opportunity, we're left in emotional limbo—writing the ending ourselves with fragments of what we know, and far too much of what we don't.

We sit with unanswered questions:

- Did I matter?
- Why didn't they say goodbye?
- Was it something I did?

These questions loop in our minds, making the silence feel louder, heavier. But over time, I learned this: their silence is not a reflection of your worth. It is often a mirror of their capacity—or lack thereof. It says more about their emotional limitations than your value as a human being.

The hard part is, our hearts are wired for connection. We crave closure because we want to understand, to soothe the ache, to put the pieces of the puzzle back together. But closure doesn't always arrive tied up in clarity. Sometimes, it comes wrapped in confusion, and we have to choose peace anyway.

# When People Disappear

Sometimes people leave without explanation because they lack the emotional tools to do otherwise. It doesn't mean you were unimportant. It means they couldn't meet you in the depth you offered. And while that hurts, accepting this truth is a radical act of self-respect.

When we stop needing closure from someone who couldn't show up with honesty or integrity, we reclaim our power. We stop waiting. We stop writing chapters for someone who never showed up on the page.

And that is a turning point: when you realize you no longer need their words to feel whole. When you start validating your own emotions. When you realize that someone else's inability to close the door properly doesn't mean you're not allowed to walk through it and move forward.

You deserve peace. Even when someone else couldn't give you the decency of a proper goodbye.

## When Death Comes Too Soon

Sudden loss brings its own kind of grief. There's no chance for parting words, no final hug, no resolution. You're left holding so much love with nowhere to place it. And the silence? It echoes. It hurts in a different way.

But maybe goodbye isn't always about words. Maybe it's about presence. About honoring what was and allowing yourself to feel it all—the love, the sorrow, the gratitude, the longing.

Speak your truth aloud. Write the letter you never got to send. Light the candle. Hold their photo. Visit the place. Say goodbye in a way that brings your soul peace—even if they're not physically here to hear it.

Because that act of expression, that honoring, is sacred.

And if you need a little more permission to grieve without answers, here it is: You are allowed to miss them and move forward. You are allowed to honor them and still feel angry. Love and grief are not opposites. They are companions.

## Self-Created Closure

Closure is not a gift someone else gives you. It's a boundary you build for yourself. It's the decision to stop bleeding for someone who stopped showing up. It's the quiet courage to say, "This chapter is over, and I deserve to move on."

Here are a few gentle ways to create your own closure:

- **Write the Unsent Letter:** Say everything that was left unsaid. Don't hold back. Let it pour out of you.
- **Create a Ritual:** Burn the letter, bury a token, take a walk with intention. Symbolically mark the end of the chapter.
- **Speak Your Goodbye Aloud:** Find a safe space and give your voice to your truth. Let your words be heard by the universe.
- **Practice Forgiveness:** Not to excuse, but to unchain your heart. Forgiveness is for you, not for them.
- **Affirm Your Worth:** Look yourself in the mirror and say, "I mattered. I always did. And I choose peace now."

This is your healing. You don't need their permission to begin. You don't need their acknowledgment to find your strength. You don't need their closure to create your own.

## **Moving Forward Without the Final Word**

You may never get the apology, the explanation, or the closure you hoped for. But you can still heal. You can still grow. You can still open your heart to love and life again.

Because healing isn't about perfect endings. It's about choosing peace in the midst of imperfection. It's about knowing that your worth is not dependent on someone else's ability to recognize it.

You don't need their goodbye to begin your new chapter.

You are worthy of healing. You are worthy of peace. You are worthy of a life that doesn't keep waiting on someone else's final word.

So say your goodbye in your own time, in your own way. Cry if you need to. Scream if you must. Then breathe. Rest. And know this:

**You didn't need their closure to heal.**

**You were the closure all along.**

**Affirmation to Anchor This Chapter:** "I release the need for answers from those who couldn't give them. I create closure within myself. I am worthy of peace, even in the absence of goodbye."

# PART 2
# HEALING, TRUTH & TRANSFORMATION

# Chapter 9:
# Betrayal, Lies, and the Beautiful Mess of Healing

*"Sometimes the strongest thing you can do
is stop explaining yourself and start walking away"*
— **Unknown**

In life, there's the truth you uncover within yourself—and then there's the truth that crashes in from the outside, often without warning. Betrayal delivers that second kind. It shows up like an unwelcome guest, kicking down the door of your peace, rearranging everything you thought you knew. One moment, you're standing on solid ground; the next, you're reeling in the rubble of someone else's deception.

And you wonder, How did I not see this coming?

But betrayal isn't about your blindness or naiveté. It's about the other person's inability to live authentically, to tell the truth, to honor your humanity. Accepting this truth is painful, yes—but it's also liberating. Because once you stop clinging to the illusion of who you thought they were, you begin the sacred process of reclaiming your power.

## The Lies We Tell Ourselves

Denial is our first defense mechanism. It cushions the blow when the truth feels too big to hold:

- "Maybe it's not as bad as it seems."
- "They didn't mean to hurt me."
- "If I just love them harder, it will get better."

These stories protect us—temporarily. But they also keep us stuck. They delay our healing. They keep us spinning in a loop of hope and hurt. And they erode our trust in ourselves.

One of the greatest acts of self-love is to stop explaining away someone else's betrayal and to start listening to the quiet truth inside of you—the one that says, This isn't okay.

We often think loyalty means staying, even when our needs are unmet, even when we're being harmed. But real loyalty? It starts with ourselves. With the vow to honor our boundaries, to believe what we feel, and to walk away when our soul whispers, "this is not love."

## The Moment of Reckoning

There comes a moment—sometimes sudden, sometimes gradual—when you can no longer pretend. When the truth is undeniable, and the pain of staying the same outweighs the fear of letting go. That moment is sacred. It stings, but it frees you.

Because once the veil lifts, you can stop negotiating your boundaries. You can stop begging for breadcrumbs of love. You can stop trying to be enough for someone who was never willing to meet you where you were.

This is the point where your healing begins—not when they apologize or come back, but when you stop waiting for them to.

And let's be honest: even if they did come back, the damage has already been done. The trust is fractured. The version of you that tolerated it? You evolving. You not available for half-truths or emotional acrobatics anymore. You wants peace. You deserves peace.

## A Catalyst for Growth

Betrayal, as brutal as it is, can become a catalyst. It forces you to examine your needs, your values, and your relationship with yourself. You start asking different questions:

- What do I truly deserve?
- What parts of me have I been silencing to keep the peace?
- What boundaries need to be built or rebuilt?
- How can I trust myself again?

It's not about building walls. It's about choosing relationships that honor your truth, your energy, and your evolution.

Healing after betrayal isn't linear. Some days you'll feel strong. Other days, the grief will sneak back in through unexpected triggers—a song, a scent, a memory. Be gentle with yourself. Grief and healing can coexist.

## The Role of Self-Compassion

Healing from betrayal requires radical self-compassion. Not the kind that glosses over the pain—but the kind that sits with it, cradles it, and says, You didn't deserve this. And you're going to be okay.

Here are a few supportive practices to nurture your healing:

- **Write the Letter You'll Never Send:** Let it all out—the rage, the grief, the confusion. Say what you need to say, for you.

- **Practice Grounding:** When the emotions surge, anchor into your body. Breathe deeply. Feel your feet on the earth. Remind yourself: I am safe now.

- **Reinforce Your Boundaries:** Get crystal clear on what you will and won't accept moving forward. Boundaries are not walls—they're bridges to your self-worth.

- **Affirm Your Truth:** Remind yourself daily: "I did nothing to deserve dishonesty. I am worthy of safe, loving, honest connections."

You don't have to rush this process. You don't have to pretend you're fine. Just keep showing up for yourself, one small moment at a time. Let the grief have its voice, but don't let it drive. Let the healing be messy and nonlinear and human.

## Releasing Bitterness to Reclaim Joy

Forgiveness is not about excusing what happened. It's about setting yourself free. It's saying: You no longer get to live rent-free in my heart.

It's releasing the grip of bitterness so you can make room for joy again. For peace. For lightness.

And yes, you're allowed to laugh at the absurdity of it all. Humor won't erase the betrayal—but it can make the weight a little easier to carry. It reminds you that you're still here, still capable of joy, still able to feel something other than pain.

You've survived the betrayal. That in itself is no small thing. But more than that—you've begun to heal. To rebuild. To remember your worth.

You are not the story someone else wrote through their betrayal. You are the author of what comes next.

So go ahead: Rebuild. Reinvent. Reinforce your boundaries. Rewrite the narrative. Not because you have to prove anything—but because you finally know your worth.

This isn't the end of your story. It's the beginning of your comeback.

**Because you are not defined by what broke you. You are defined by how beautifully you rise.**

**Affirmation to Anchor This Chapter:** "I release the hold betrayal had on my heart. I trust myself again. I honor the truth I carry, and I choose peace, healing, and joy from this day forward."

# Chapter 10:

# Perfection vs. Reality: Why Embracing the Mess Leads to True Happiness

*"Perfection is not attainable, but if we chase perfection, we can catch excellence."*
— **Vince Lombardi**

We live in a world that constantly whispers (and often shouts), "Be perfect." We're surrounded by curated highlight reels, polished captions, and seemingly flawless lives. Social media becomes a gallery of perfection—posed family photos, color-coordinated closets, effortless success stories. It's easy to start believing that anything less than flawless isn't good enough.

But beneath the filters and the staged smiles, real life is happening. And it's gloriously, beautifully messy. And real life—that's where the magic is.

## The Trap of "Perfect" Living

Perfection is seductive. It promises peace if you can just do it all right. Be the perfect parent, partner, coach, yogi, entrepreneur. It tells you that happiness lives just beyond the next achievement, just after you lose ten pounds, just after your house looks like a Pinterest board.

But here's the truth: perfection is a moving target. Just when you think you've arrived, the bar shifts. It's a game you can't win—and one that robs you of the joy found in the now.

Perfection is rigid. Reality is flexible. Perfection demands. Reality invites. Perfection says, "Be better." Reality says, "Be here."

And here? Here is where we feel, learn, grow, stumble, and rise again. Here is where we become whole.

## The Reality Check We All Need

Reality humbles us—and thank goodness it does. You set intentions for a mindful morning and spill your smoothie on your journal. You commit to inner peace, then lose your patience in traffic. You preach balance, then burn out. Welcome to being human.

Perfection screams, "You're failing." Reality whispers, "You're growing."

You don't need ideal conditions to begin. Life isn't holding its breath until you get it together. It's unfolding right now—inviting you to participate, not perform.

It's taken me years to realize that my mess doesn't disqualify me from guiding others—it actually makes me more relatable. It shows that I walk this path too. That healing, growth, and evolution are never tidy. And that sometimes, the most powerful lessons come from the days that didn't go as planned.

## Embracing Imperfection in Practice

I've stumbled out of yoga poses. I've eaten ice cream straight from the carton after preaching conscious eating. I've had weeks where my to-do list won. None of that makes me a fraud. It makes me real.

Each misstep reminds me I'm not here to impress—I'm here to experience. To evolve. To be fully alive.

When we stop pretending to have it all figured out, we give others permission to do the same. That's where real connection lives—in our shared humanity, not our polished masks.

Let's face it: perfection is lonely. Vulnerability is where the light gets in. And when we allow ourselves to be seen—mess and all—we begin to heal not just ourselves, but each other.

## From Perfection to Progress

Letting go of perfection doesn't mean lowering your standards. It means shifting your focus—from outcome to effort, from flawlessness to authenticity.

You start to:

- Celebrate the 5-minute meditation instead of berating yourself for skipping an hour.
- Honor your courage for starting, even if you're unsure.
- Appreciate the little wins—the boundaries set, the deep breath taken, the tear finally allowed.

Progress is quiet. It happens in inches, not leaps. But it's powerful.

And guess what? Progress is sustainable. Perfection is not.

## Practical Steps to Embrace the Mess

- **Acknowledge the Illusion:** Remind yourself daily—social media is not real life. It's a highlight reel, not the full story.
- **Practice Self-Compassion:** When you mess up (because you will), speak to yourself like you would a beloved friend. Gentle. Kind. Encouraging.
- **Celebrate Small Wins:** Every small choice made in alignment matters. They build the life you want.
- **Get Comfortable with Discomfort:** Growth is messy. Let it be. Let yourself be new at things. Let yourself be awkward. That's where magic begins.
- **Find Humor in the Imperfection:** Laugh when your smoothie explodes or when you say the wrong thing. Laughter softens the edges of self-judgment.

## You Are Enough—Right Now

Perfection will always try to run the show. But you get to choose whether you let it.

Your worth isn't found in a perfect image. It's found in your honesty. In your resilience. In your willingness to keep showing up, even when it's hard. Especially when it's hard.

So let's make a pact: Next time perfection knocks, pause. Take a breath. Smile at the mess. And say, "Not today."

Because your life—your imperfect, beautiful, real life—is more than enough.

And in the end, it's not about being flawless. It's about being free.

## Affirmation to Anchor This Chapter:

"I release the need to be perfect. I welcome my humanity, my flaws, and my growth. I am enough, just as I am—and becoming more of myself every day.

# Chapter 11:
# Say Goodbye to Self-Doubt: Overcoming Imposter Syndrome and Embracing Your True Power

*"Our deepest fear is not that we are inadequate. Our deepest fear is that we are powerful beyond measure."*
**— Marianne Williamson**

Have you ever achieved something incredible—a promotion, a personal milestone, a powerful breakthrough—only to hear a voice in your head whisper, "You're a fraud. You just got lucky. They're going to figure you out"?

If so, welcome to the very human experience of imposter syndrome.

Despite external evidence of success, imposter syndrome has a way of shrinking us. It convinces us we're pretending, that we've fooled everyone, that we don't really belong in the room. But here's the truth: You do belong. You did earn it. And it's time to stop handing the mic to that fear and start embracing your full, radiant power—with a little humor and grace along the way.

## What Is Imposter Syndrome?

Imposter syndrome is the sneaky, persistent feeling that you're not as competent, talented, or deserving as others think you are. It's the belief that your success is luck, timing, or smoke and mirrors.

It's rooted in perfectionism, self-doubt, and the false belief that everyone else has it figured out but you. Spoiler alert: they don't.

## Spotting the Symptoms

Imposter syndrome can be subtle—or loud. Here's how it might show up:

- You downplay your achievements: "It wasn't a big deal."
- You reject compliments: "Anyone could have done it."
- You feel like you're faking it: "They're going to realize I don't know what I'm doing."

If you nodded yes to any of these, don't worry—you're in good company. The key is recognizing it so you can begin to rewrite the narrative.

## Reframe Your Inner Dialogue

That critical inner voice? It's like an outdated software program running on fear. Time for an upgrade.

Try this:

- When you think, "I'm not good enough," replace it with, "I'm growing, evolving, and doing my best."

When you think, "I'm going to fail," try, "I'm learning something valuable, no matter the outcome."

Affirmation to Anchor You: I am worthy of my success. I've earned my place. I bring unique gifts to the world.

## Own Your Achievements

Stop giving luck all the credit. Your success is not a fluke.

Take inventory:

- What did you overcome?
- What bold steps did you take?
- What habits, boundaries, or risks led to this win?

Celebrate yourself. You didn't get here by accident. You showed up, you did the work, and you rose.

## Embrace the Learning Process

Perfectionism is imposter syndrome's favorite fuel. But life isn't a test with all the answers—it's a process. You're allowed to evolve, to change your mind, to not know everything.

Mindset Shift: Replace "I should already know this" with "I'm here to grow."

Mistakes aren't failures. They're proof that you're trying, stretching, expanding. And that's exactly what growth looks like.

## Stop the Comparison Game

Comparison is the thief of joy—and the amplifier of imposter syndrome.

Social media is a highlight reel, not a behind-the-scenes documentary. You're comparing your full humanity to someone else's edited storyline. It's not fair, and it's not real.

Instead, focus on your own lane. Celebrate your progress. Your pace is perfect for your path.

## Visualize Success

Visualization isn't fluff—it's fuel. Mentally rehearsing success builds confidence. Close your eyes and picture yourself speaking, leading, thriving. Feel it. Own it.

The more you see yourself succeeding, the more your nervous system gets on board with that truth.

## Lean on Your Support System

You're not meant to carry this alone. Share your fears with someone safe. Surround yourself with people who reflect your light when you forget it's there.

Mentors, coaches, friends—they remind you of your brilliance when your inner critic gets loud.

## Practice Self-Compassion

You are human. You will have off days. You will feel insecure. That's not a flaw—it's part of the deal.

Speak gently to yourself. Rest when needed. Celebrate what you did right. Healing from imposter syndrome doesn't happen in one aha moment. It happens in consistent, daily reminders that you are enough.

## Embrace Your Power

Imposter syndrome may not disappear completely. But it doesn't get to drive the bus anymore. You've got goals. A mission. A story to tell.

Your success is real. Your voice matters. Your presence is needed.

So take the next step. Speak up. Apply for the thing. Launch the idea. Say yes to the opportunity. Not because you're perfect—but because you're ready.

Because you're not here to shrink. You're here to rise.

# Chapter 12:

# Reason, Season, Lifetime: Knowing When to Let Go and When to Hold On

*"People come into your life for a reason, a season, or a lifetime."*
**— Unknown**

There's a quiet rhythm to life that only becomes clear when we pause long enough—or hurt deeply enough—to look back. In those reflective moments, we begin to understand that not every person, pursuit, or path is meant to stay with us forever. And the wisdom lies in learning to let go when it's time—and hold on when it's right.

I used to fight the endings. I would grip tightly to people, projects, and passions, afraid of what their departure might mean about me. If something ended, I feared I had failed. But I've learned that endings aren't failures. They're transitions. And often, they are the space-making grace that allows something truer to emerge.

## Understanding the Roles

Some people and experiences are here for a reason—to teach us, to challenge us, to stretch us in ways we didn't ask for but ultimately needed. These are the catalysts. The wake-up calls. The ones who push us toward our purpose, often without realizing it.

Others show up for a season—a brief but beautiful chapter. They may bring joy, passion, heartbreak, or momentum. They walk with us for a while, and then life nudges us in different directions. Their purpose is not permanence—it's presence during a specific stretch of our journey.

And then there are the lifetimes. The people and paths that ground us, grow with us, and remain, even as the world around us shifts. These are the rare, sacred ones. They are the friendships that feel like home. The passions that evolve alongside us. The callings that continue to light us up year after year.

Sometimes, we try to force a reason into a season, or a season into a lifetime. We fight to keep something alive that's already run its course, pouring energy into trying to resurrect a chapter that has already closed. It's human. It's tender. And yet, when we hold on too tightly, we can't receive what's trying to arrive.

## Letting Go with Grace

I used to panic when a season ended. I tried to stretch things out past their natural timeline—clinging to what felt familiar, even when it no longer fit. Tennis was one of those seasons. What started as joy turned into pressure, burnout, and guilt. I held on too long, thinking if I just tried harder, I could recapture the spark. But some things aren't meant to last forever. And the beauty is—they don't have to.

Letting go isn't giving up. It's honoring the cycle. It's choosing flow over force. It's trusting that release creates space for something new. Sometimes, what we're letting go of isn't even the thing itself—it's the story we attached to it. The identity it gave us. The comfort it provided. And releasing that can feel like a mini-death—a shedding. But with every shedding comes renewal.

Letting go doesn't always come with closure. Sometimes you don't get the neat ending or the clear goodbye. Sometimes you simply wake up and know it's time. You feel it in your bones. And when you trust that knowing, you make space for alignment. For peace. For what's next.

## Recognizing the Gifts

When you look back on your own journey, what chapters have closed, even though you tried to keep them open?

Was it a job you once loved but quietly outgrew? A friendship that began to fade as your values shifted? A version of yourself that no longer reflects who you are becoming?

It takes courage to release what we've outgrown. But it's in the releasing that we find our next layer of freedom.

Recognizing the difference between a reason, a season, and a lifetime changes everything. It brings peace. It softens the sting of goodbye. It helps us loosen our grip on what no longer serves us—and treasure what truly matters.

You can love someone deeply and still know they were only meant to walk part of your path. You can honor a passion or a project and still know it's time to pivot. That's not abandonment—it's alignment.

## Lifetimes That Sustain You

The lifetimes—those are your anchors. They are your people, your sacred callings, your north stars. These are the ones who walk beside you through your mess and your magic, who celebrate your wins and hold space for your tears.

They are the ones you can call at 2 a.m. and the ones who challenge you with love when you forget your worth. These relationships are rare, and they are worthy of your deepest care.

These are also the parts of your soul work that evolve with you. Your callings. Your dharma. The work that keeps whispering to you, even as everything else changes. When you find your lifetimes, you'll feel it in your nervous system. Safe. Energized. Alive.

Nourish them. Show up for them. And if you haven't found them yet, trust—they are out there, seeking you too.

## Your Call to Reflect

Take a breath and gently ask yourself:

- Who or what have I been trying to make a "lifetime" when it was really a season?
- What am I ready to release, not in bitterness, but in gratitude?
- What relationships or callings are asking to be honored more deeply?
- Where in my life am I clinging instead of flowing?

You don't have to have all the answers. Just let the questions sit with you. Journal on them. Walk with them. Let them guide you into clarity.

And remember: clarity often comes in whispers, not in declarations. It arrives when we're quiet enough to hear it.

## Trusting the Unfolding

When we understand the roles people and experiences play in our lives, we stop forcing things to fit. We stop clinging out of fear. And we begin to move with the current of our lives rather than against it.

Reason. Season. Lifetime. Each has its place. Each offers a sacred gift.

Your job isn't to hold on to everything. It's to hold on to what aligns—and release what doesn't, with love.

Because the more you trust the rhythm, the more space you create for the people, paths, and passions that are meant to walk with you for the long haul.

And that? That is a life lived in harmony with your truth.

## Soul Reminder:

"Some chapters end not because they weren't beautiful, but because you are now being called to write something even truer. Trust the pen in your hand."

# Chapter 13:

# The Comfort in Discomfort: Why We Stay Too Long

*"We don't fear the unknown. We fear what we project onto it."*
— **Deepak Chopra**

Why do we stay in relationships, jobs, habits, and environments that we know—deep down—aren't right for us anymore?

Because leaving means stepping into the unknown. And the unknown can feel like a vast, echoing void. Uncertainty often masquerades as danger, and as humans, we are wired to seek comfort, familiarity, and safety. Even when that comfort is wrapped in dysfunction or quiet disappointment, it feels easier than risking what we can't see.

I've stayed too long before. I've clung to comfort, to potential, to dreams that were fading but not quite gone. I've convinced myself I just needed more time, more patience, more effort. And I've laid awake in the dark, wrestling with the question, "What if I let go and nothing better comes?"

But here's what I've learned: The fear of the unknown isn't the enemy. The real danger is abandoning yourself to avoid it.

## Comfort Isn't Always Safe

Just because something is familiar doesn't mean it's meant for you. Predictable pain is still pain. Routine struggle is still struggle.

We confuse the safety of the known with the security of the right path. But there's nothing secure about shrinking to fit a life that no longer fits you.

Real safety comes from within. It comes from knowing you can handle whatever comes next. It comes from trusting your ability to navigate change, to feel discomfort, and to keep going.

Fear will whisper, "What if it's worse out there?" Growth will ask, "But what if it's better?"

And here's the wild thing: even if it isn't better right away, it will still be worth it—because you'll be living from truth, not fear. You'll be walking in alignment, not in circles.

## The Psychological Traps That Keep Us Stuck

There are deep-rooted beliefs that hold us in place, even when everything inside us is asking for change:

- Attachment wounds that make letting go feel like abandonment, not liberation.
- Self-doubt that convinces us we're not strong enough to leap.
- Hopeful fantasies that keep us chasing potential instead of accepting reality.
- Guilt that says we're selfish for wanting more, for wanting different.

These are not truths. They are survival strategies dressed in logic. They once protected you. They got you through hard things. But now they are the cage, not the key.

You can do hard things. You've done them before. You are allowed to outgrow people, places, and patterns. You are allowed to walk away—not because you gave up, but because you woke up.

## Courage Isn't the Absence of Fear—It's Action in Spite of It

Leaving something that is "fine" for something that is right is an act of deep courage. It doesn't have to be loud or dramatic. Sometimes, it's a quiet decision made in the solitude of your own heart—a soft but powerful "no more."

That small act of truth becomes your turning point. Your reclamation. Your path back to yourself.

Courage is saying, "I choose the unknown because I believe something better exists—because I believe I am worthy of finding it."

When we walk toward uncertainty with intention and self-compassion, life often meets us with unexpected grace. Doors open. Guides appear. We realize we were never walking alone.

And even when fear travels with us, we don't have to let it lead. We can acknowledge it, thank it for trying to protect us, and keep moving forward.

## A Journal Prompt for Your Journey

Ask yourself honestly:

- What am I afraid will happen if I let go?
- What might happen if I don't?
- What do I believe I'll lose—and what might I gain?

Let the answers rise without judgment. Fear is not a stop sign—it's a signal. It's data. It tells you where your edge is. It's there to be honored, but not obeyed.

## Your Next Step

What would it look like to take just one small step out of your comfort zone today? Not a leap. Not a grand declaration. Just a single, soul-aligned action.

Maybe it's:

- Having a vulnerable conversation.
- Writing down the truth you've been avoiding.
- Decluttering one item that represents an old chapter.

- Saying "yes" to something that excites you (and scares you).

Maybe it's simply saying to yourself: I'm ready to live with more truth than fear.

The unknown is only scary until you arrive. Then it becomes your new normal. Your new strength. Your new beginning.

And more often than not, what's waiting for you on the other side of fear is not danger—it's freedom. Freedom to trust your intuition. Freedom to write your own narrative. Freedom to breathe fully again.

So take a breath. Take a step. And remember:

You are not walking into the void. You are walking home to yourself.

# PART 3

# EMBODIMENT & EMPOWERMENT

## Chapter 14:

# How Vulnerability Unlocks Emotional Strength and Authentic Connections

*"Vulnerability sounds like truth and feels like courage. Truth and courage aren't always comfortable, but they're never weakness."*
— **Brené Brown**

There was a time when I believed vulnerability was weakness—a crack in my armor that made me look soft, unstable, or less capable. I thought being strong meant being unshakable. So I built walls. High ones. Thick ones. I smiled through pain. I said "I'm fine" when I wasn't. I was determined to be the strong one—the one who didn't need anything from anyone.

But over time, that armor didn't feel like strength. It felt like suffocation.

Here's the truth I've come to know: vulnerability doesn't make you weak. It makes you honest. And honesty is the foundation of every authentic relationship—including the one you have with yourself.

## The Armor We Wear

Most of us wear some form of emotional armor. We polish our social masks, edit our words, and carefully curate our public selves. We do it to feel safe. To be accepted. To avoid judgment.

But the cost of that protection? Disconnection.

That armor may keep out criticism, but it also keeps out intimacy. It may protect your pride, but it prevents people from loving the real you. Over time, it creates distance—not only from others, but from your own truth.

We become strangers to our own feelings, numbing the parts that feel too tender to touch. And we wonder why we feel alone, even in a crowded room.

## Letting Yourself Be Seen

I remember the first time I let someone see me fully. Not the version of me that was polished or impressive—but the one that was scared and unsure. I braced for judgment. What I received was grace.

That moment changed me.

Vulnerability is not about dramatic oversharing. It's about brave honesty. It's the courage to say:

- "I need help."
- "I don't know what I'm doing."

- "I'm scared, but I'm trying."
- "I care deeply, and I'm afraid to lose this."

It's the choice to let someone into your reality—even when your voice shakes. And yes, it's risky. You can't control how people will respond. But when you find the ones who meet you with empathy, understanding, and care—it's pure magic. That's where true, soul-nourishing connection lives.

## Strength Isn't Stoic—It's Soft

We've been taught that strength looks like stoicism. That holding it together is noble. But true strength is expansive, not rigid. It's allowing space for your truth. It's the quiet, powerful act of being real.

Strength is:

- Admitting when you're tired.
- Asking for help.
- Owning your emotions without apology.
- Speaking your truth, even when it's messy.

When we allow ourselves to be vulnerable, we offer others permission to do the same. We become safe places. Mirrors. Bridges.

Vulnerability is contagious—and in the best way.

## Connection Over Perfection

Perfection is isolating. It says, "I've got this all figured out." Vulnerability says, "I'm doing my best, just like you."

And that's what brings us closer.

You don't have to be flawless to be loved. In fact, it's your softness, your imperfections, and your willingness to be seen that allow others to find themselves in you.

You don't need to impress—you need to be present. You don't need to hide—you need to open. Just a little. Just enough.

## A Loving Challenge

Think of someone in your life who sees the "put-together" version of you. The one who always says, "I'm good."

What would it look like to let them see a little more?

- Could you share something vulnerable?
- Could you admit a fear?
- Could you ask for support, even just a listening ear?

Vulnerability isn't about being weak—it's about being whole. It's about living with your heart open, even when it's easier to shut it down.

## Your Invitation

If you've been living behind walls, here's your invitation: start opening the door. Not to everyone. Not all at once. But in the spaces where you long for deeper connection—begin there.

**Let someone in. Let yourself out.**

Because vulnerability is not your weakness—it's your superpower. It's your bridge to authentic relationships, soulful alignment, and the kind of emotional strength that transforms everything it touches.

Start small. Start now.

You are safe to be seen.

## Chapter 15:

# Crossing the Threshold: Where Fear Meets Growth

---

*"You can only lose what you cling to."*
**— Buddha**

Let's talk about the limbo zone—the sacred space between what was and what could be. The waiting room of life. The place where you know something needs to change, but fear of the unknown has its grip on your soul, whispering, But what if it's worse than what you have now?

I've lived in that space. I've paced its floors, replayed every what-if, and clung to the comfort of the familiar, even when it was draining the life out of me. Relationships that no longer nurtured me. Jobs that stifled my spirit. Identities that felt like old clothes—too tight, too worn.

And why did I stay? Because the future was foggy. Because the discomfort I knew felt safer than the possibility of something unknown.

But here's the sacred truth: comfort isn't always where we thrive.

## Why We Stay

We stay in jobs that no longer inspire us. In relationships that feel hollow. In patterns that no longer reflect who we are. Not because we're broken—but because we're human.

Our nervous system craves certainty. Our minds want guarantees. We want to know the ending before we turn the page. And life? Life doesn't work that way.

So we stall. We justify. We rehearse worst-case scenarios, convincing ourselves it's better to stay where we are than risk the unknown.

But here's the truth we forget: safety without growth is a slow kind of suffering. We trade vitality for predictability. Joy for familiarity. Expansion for ease.

## The Fear Beneath the Fear

At its core, fear of the unknown isn't about the future. It's about what we fear we won't be able to feel if it doesn't go our way:

- Disappointment
- Rejection
- Grief
- Loneliness

But you've already felt those things—and you're still here. You survived them. You learned from them. And if life brings them again, you'll survive those too.

What if the unknown isn't a threat, but an invitation? What if the discomfort is a bridge—to something more aligned, more soulful, more you?

## When You're at the Edge

Standing at the edge of change is rarely graceful. It's shaky. Tender. Full of doubt.

You question everything. You stall. You bargain. You panic. And then one day—you leap.

Sometimes because you're inspired. Sometimes because you're broken open. But often? Because you're finally tired of staying small.

And that's when the shift begins. That's when the fog begins to part.

## From Surviving to Trusting

The unknown softens when you begin to trust yourself. Not trust that things will go perfectly—but trust that no matter how they go, you've got you.

You begin to understand: you don't need the whole map. Just the courage to take the next small step. And then the next.

Progress rarely looks like a breakthrough. It often looks like:

- A quiet decision.
- A whispered truth.
- A boundary gently set.
- A moment of stillness where you choose not to abandon yourself.

That's where life changes.

## Your Turn to Choose

Ask yourself gently:

- What am I afraid of losing?
- What am I afraid of feeling?
- What might I gain if I let go?

Write it down. Sit with it. Let the truth rise.

Then ask: What's one small act of bravery I can take today?

Maybe it's sending the email.

Maybe it's speaking the truth.

Maybe it's admitting, "I don't want this anymore."

Remember: you don't need to leap. You just need to move. One breath. One step. One truth at a time.

## The Beautiful Truth

Everything meaningful in my life—the growth, the healing, the relationships that anchor me—came from stepping into the unknown. Not one of them came from staying comfortable.

And yes, I still feel fear. We all do. But I've learned to walk with it, hand in hand. I've learned to trust that even in the dark, I'm still being guided.

So are you.

You don't have to have it all figured out. You don't need certainty to take a step. You just need to trust the deeper knowing inside of you that says:

There's more for me than this.

Take the step. Breathe through the fog. Let the next version of you meet you on the other side.

Your future isn't waiting for you to be fearless. It's waiting for you to be faithful—to yourself.

# Chapter 16:

# Vulnerability as a Superpower—The Gateway to True Connection

*"Vulnerability is the birthplace of innovation, creativity, and change."*
**— Brené Brown**

For the longest time, I wore strength like armor. I had perfected the art of appearing composed—smiling through uncertainty, offering support while secretly needing it myself, pretending everything was fine while holding pain just beneath the surface.

Like many of us, I believed vulnerability was weakness. Something to manage. To hide. To apologize for. I thought if I let people see my wounds, they'd see me as fragile. But life has a way of stripping away those illusions.

Over time, I softened. Or maybe, more truthfully, I cracked. And in that cracking, I discovered the truth: Vulnerability isn't weakness—it's the birthplace of strength. It's the key to everything real.

## Why We Hide

From an early age, we're taught to be "strong," but that strength is often code for suppression.

- Don't cry.
- Don't let them see you struggle.
- Don't admit when you're scared.

So we build emotional walls. We become masters of the highlight reel. We smile through sadness, keep quiet in conflict, and carry the weight alone.

We fear that if people see the real us—messy, emotional, uncertain—they'll leave. But here's the paradox: The very thing we think will push people away is what draws them closest.

When you say, "This is what I'm going through," when you admit, "I don't have it all figured out," when you let someone see you as you are—you create space for them to be real, too. And in that shared space? Walls fall. Hearts soften. Authentic connection begins.

## Vulnerability Is Connection

Every deep, soul-nourishing relationship I've ever had—whether personal or professional—was rooted in vulnerability. It's what takes connection from surface to soul. It's what turns strangers into kindred spirits. It's what transforms coaching from transactional to transformational.

And yes, vulnerability carries risk. You might open your heart and be met with silence. You might share your truth and be misunderstood. But even then—you've chosen honesty over hiding. You've honored yourself. And that is never a mistake.

## The Strength Behind the Softness

There's a fierce kind of strength in saying, "This is me." Not a version crafted for approval. Not a persona curated for applause. Just you—honest, imperfect, whole.

Vulnerability is also how we heal. When we stop numbing, stop pretending, and allow ourselves to feel—really feel—we begin to mend the places we've been carrying pain in silence.

That moment when you say, "I'm not okay," is often the moment everything starts to shift. Because the truth is: your softness doesn't make you fragile. It makes you real. And real is where the power lives.

## Permission to Be Real

Let this chapter be your permission slip:

- You don't have to be the strong one all the time.
- You don't have to hold it all together.
- You don't have to hide your heart.

In fact, the more you lead with truth, the more the right people—your people—will show up. Not the ones who love the performance. The ones who love the person.

Vulnerability is a filter. It reveals who can meet you in your depth—and who can't. And that clarity is a gift.

## Small Acts of Courage

Vulnerability doesn't always look like a grand confession. Often, it's a quiet act of courage in the everyday:

- Saying, "I need help."
- Telling someone, "I'm scared, but I'm trying."
- Letting someone in after being hurt before.
- Owning a mistake instead of hiding it.
- Saying, "I care about you," even without certainty it will be returned.

Each moment is a choice—a brave step toward freedom.

## A World Changed by Courage

Imagine what might shift if you chose to be just a little more open. A little more honest. A little more willing to let the mask drop.

What might heal? What might deepen? What new connection could bloom?

Vulnerability isn't about oversharing. It's about being aligned. It's about showing up—imperfect and real—and letting that be enough.

And when you do that? You don't just change your relationships. You change the world.

Because every time you choose truth over performance, you create space for someone else to do the same. And that is how we heal—together, one honest moment at a time.

**Chapter 17:**

# Into the Mystery: Finding Freedom in Letting Go

---

*"Faith is taking the first step even when you don't see the whole staircase."*
**— Martin Luther King Jr.**

There's something incredibly humbling about standing at the edge of the unknown. That liminal space between what was and what hasn't yet revealed itself. It's where we wrestle with uncertainty, anxiety, and the deep longing for clarity. It's raw. It's quiet. And sometimes, it's downright terrifying.

I've stood there many times—heart pounding, gripping tightly to what felt familiar, even if it wasn't fulfilling. Waiting for a sign. A guarantee. A plan. And what I've discovered is this: Control won't save you—but surrender will set you free.

## Why We Crave Certainty

Our brains are wired to find patterns. To seek out what's predictable, manageable, and known. Control feels safe.

It offers us the illusion that we can prevent disappointment or avoid pain.

So we try to orchestrate every outcome. We overthink. We obsess. We micromanage our lives.

We ask the same questions over and over:

- "What if it doesn't work out?"
- "What if I make the wrong choice?"
- "What if I fail?"

But life doesn't follow our scripts. It doesn't respond to our spreadsheets. It asks us to live—not to calculate.

Control is not safety—it's a cage. And the key to freedom? Trusting what we cannot yet see.

## The Discomfort of the In-Between

There is a very specific ache that comes from being between versions of yourself. Between chapters. Between relationships. Between dreams.

You've outgrown what was—but you haven't yet stepped fully into what will be.

This space? It's tender. It's frustrating. And it's wildly sacred.

It's where patience is forged. Where identity is unraveled and rebuilt. Where the old self is laid to rest, and the new self takes root—slowly, quietly, and often without fanfare.

The invitation here isn't to rush forward. It's to pause. To breathe. To trust that not everything needs to be figured out today.

Because clarity isn't always immediate—but it's always on its way.

## Letting Go Doesn't Mean Giving Up

Surrender isn't about quitting. It's about loosening your grip.

It's about doing your part—showing up, preparing, staying aligned—and then releasing the outcome. It's the willingness to say:

"I don't know how this ends… but I trust that I'll find my way."

This kind of trust isn't passive. It's active. It's choosing to live with your heart open, even without a roadmap. It's the radical act of showing up anyway.

Letting go is not giving in—it's giving up the illusion that you were ever in charge of everything to begin with. And that's not weakness. That's wisdom.

## Anchors in the Storm

When the future feels foggy, here are ways to stay grounded:

- **Create daily rituals:** Morning stillness, mindful movement, or writing can anchor you in the now.
- **Lean into community:** Talk with people who've walked similar paths. Be witnessed. Be held.
- **Listen inwardly:** Your intuition is wise. Sometimes your body knows before your mind does. Trust the quiet inner yes—or no.
- **Take aligned action:** Even small steps matter. You don't need to see the full staircase—just the next step.

And when doubt creeps in—which it will—remind yourself of all the times you've made it through the uncertain before. Make a list if you have to. You're more resilient than you think.

## The Gifts of Trust

Some of the most beautiful parts of my life came from places I didn't plan. Love I didn't expect. Healing I didn't foresee. Opportunities that showed up after I finally released what no longer aligned.

The peace I longed for didn't arrive when I figured everything out. It arrived when I stopped forcing it all to make sense.

Faith is not the absence of fear. It's the presence of grace in the midst of it. It's the choice to walk forward—even when you're trembling.

## An Invitation

If you're in a season of transition—between careers, relationships, homes, identities, or ideas—this chapter is your reminder:

It's okay to not have the answers. It's okay to be in the in-between. You are not lost. You are being re-formed.

Let go of the illusion that you must control everything. Instead, focus on who you're becoming through it all.

Because life doesn't always give us a map. Sometimes it gives us a compass.

And when you trust that inner compass, even the unknown becomes a sacred, unfolding path.

Take the step. Even if your voice shakes. Even if you don't yet know where you're going.

## Your Trust Practice

Try this:

- Light a candle in a quiet space.
- Write a letter to the version of yourself who is still clinging to control. Tell them it's safe to release. That they've done well—and it's okay to rest.
- Then, write one sentence that anchors your faith for today. Something like: "I don't know where I'm going, but I trust that I'm being guided."

Read it aloud. Breathe it in. Let it be your north star.

# Final Thoughts

You don't have to leap into the unknown all at once. You don't need all the answers to take the next step.

You just need to trust that you'll figure it out as you go. That there is wisdom in the waiting. That there is strength in surrender.

You're not falling. You're unfolding.

And what waits on the other side of the unknown? Freedom. Expansion. A deeper version of you, waiting to be met.

Take the step. Life is already reaching back.

You are safe. You are held. You are becoming.

# Chapter 18:

# The Voice Within—How to Reconnect with Your Inner Wisdom

---

*"The quieter you become, the more you can hear."*
**— Ram Dass**

In a world that glorifies noise, hustle, and constant stimulation, it's easy to forget what your own voice sounds like. Not the one you use to answer emails or show up in conversations, but the quiet, knowing voice within—the one that whispers truth, alignment, and soul-level guidance.

We scroll. We overthink. We ask for advice from ten different people. We do everything but turn inward. And yet, more often than not, the clarity we're seeking is already inside us.

Reconnecting with your inner wisdom is not a one-time event—it's a practice. A remembering. A homecoming. And like any relationship, it requires presence, patience, and deep listening.

## The Disconnection Dilemma

When life gets overwhelming, we go on autopilot. We fill every quiet moment with a screen, a task, or a distraction. Slowly, almost without realizing it, we become disconnected from our intuition.

We numb through busyness. We silence ourselves with overthinking. We trade instinct for intellect, and soul for strategy. We push through, even when something deep within us is whispering, "Pause. Reflect. There's something here for you to hear."

I've been there. Caught between what "made sense" and what felt true. I've overridden my own instincts to follow what was logical, only to find myself drained, off-path, and wondering how I ended up so far from my center.

Every time I ignored that inner nudge, I paid for it—with stress, regret, or a sense of misalignment. But when I honored it—even when it didn't make sense to anyone else—it always led me somewhere better. Somewhere truer. Somewhere home.

## The Gentle Art of Tuning In

Your inner wisdom doesn't shout. It whispers. It lives in stillness, not noise. In embodiment, not overthinking. In truth, not trend.

To hear it, we have to slow down enough to listen. We have to cultivate the quiet.

Try this:

- **Create space:** Turn off the background noise. Unplug. Be with yourself, even for five minutes.
- **Breathe deeply:** Your breath anchors you to the present. Let it soften your nervous system so your deeper truth can rise.
- **Ask, then receive:** Pose a question in your journal or heart: "What do I need right now?" Then wait. Don't force the answer. It may come as a word, an image, a sensation.
- **Follow your energy:** What expands you? What contracts you? Your body is wise. It remembers what your mind forgets.
- **Free-write:** Let your pen move without judgment. Often, your truth sneaks out between the lines.

## When You Begin to Trust Yourself

Everything shifts when you start to trust your inner knowing.

You stop outsourcing your worth to other people's opinions. You stop crowd-sourcing your truth. You begin to trust your "no" and honor your "yes."

You start asking better questions:

- What feels aligned for me?
- What does my soul need today?
- Where am I betraying myself to keep the peace?

That quiet voice—the one you used to ignore—becomes your most trusted guide. Your compass. Your anchor.

And that changes everything.

## Reclaiming Your Inner Authority

You are the expert on you. Let that sink in.

No book, coach, or guru can replace the wisdom that lives within your bones. Yes, support is beautiful. Guidance is powerful. But your life? Your path? It begins and ends with you.

The more you practice tuning in, the more confident you become in your own voice. The more you honor your inner truth, the easier it becomes to course-correct when you drift.

And you will drift. That's okay. Realignment is always available. The voice within is patient. It never leaves you—even when you stop listening.

## A Soulful Invitation

If you've been feeling lost, scattered, or out of sync, this is your invitation to come home to yourself. To return to the one voice that never left you—your own.

That voice may have been quieted by fear, drowned out by obligation, or pushed aside by logic—but it's still there. It hasn't forgotten you.

You are not broken. You are not behind. You are simply being invited to remember.

So slow down. Breathe. Listen.

Because your next step? It's already inside you.

## Inner Wisdom Practice

Try this simple evening ritual:

- Sit in a quiet space. Place your hand on your heart.
- Ask, "What truth have I been too busy to hear?"
- Breathe deeply. Wait. Listen.
- Write down whatever arises—even if it's just a feeling, an image, or a single word.

Repeat nightly. Let it become a bridge back to yourself.

## Final Thoughts

You don't need more noise. You need more trust. You don't need to be told what to do. You need to listen to what you already know.

Because the most powerful guidance doesn't come from outside of you. It comes from within.

And that voice? It's been waiting.

Come home.

# Chapter 19:

# Redefining Success—What It Really Means to Win at Life

---

*"Success is liking yourself, liking what you do, and liking how you do it."*
— **Maya Angelou**

What if success had nothing to do with how much you've achieved—and everything to do with how aligned you feel?

What if it wasn't about your title, your to-do list, your income, or your perfectly curated schedule?

What if it was about how you feel when you wake up in the morning? About whether your days are guided by intention, not obligation? About ending your day not with exhaustion—but with a quiet sense of joy, knowing you honored yourself?

For years, I thought success was about output—how much I could get done, how polished I could look doing it, and how others perceived me. I chased productivity. I clung to the hustle. I wore "busy" like a badge of honor. And while the world may have applauded, my soul was depleted.

Until one day, I stopped asking, "What more can I do?" and started asking, "What actually matters?"

## Success Isn't One-Size-Fits-All

We live in a world obsessed with performance. Success is measured by numbers—bank accounts, likes, followers, accolades. But chasing external markers of validation is a race that never ends. You reach one milestone, and the next one is already waiting. The finish line keeps moving.

But real success? It's not a race. It's a rhythm. A relationship with your life.

It's how you feel about yourself when no one's watching. It's how well your life fits your truth—not someone else's expectations. It's knowing that you're honoring what lights you up—even if it makes no sense to anyone else.

Success that's externally defined will always leave you seeking. Success that's internally defined will always lead you home.

## The Shift from Hustle to Harmony

I used to believe that slowing down meant I was falling behind. That if I wasn't constantly grinding, I was failing. But I've learned:

- Peace is productive.
- Rest is necessary.

- Joy is a compass.
- Alignment is wealth.

Success, for me now, looks very different. It includes:

- Boundaries that protect my peace
- Clients who are deeply aligned, not just profitable
- Creative time that fuels me, not drains me
- Choosing truth over performance
- Prioritizing presence over perfection

It's not about proving. It's about honoring. It's not about doing more—it's about doing what matters most.

I've traded hustle for harmony. Productivity for purpose. The applause of others for the quiet knowing of my own heart.

## Redefining on Your Own Terms

So let me ask you: **What would success look like if no one else was watching?**

Would you still be chasing what you're chasing? Would you still say yes to every demand, every opportunity, every expectation?

Or would you pivot toward what truly lights you up?

Would you:

- Choose more time in nature?
- Say no to the things that drain you?

- Start that project that's been whispering to your soul?
- Leave the path that's "safe" and follow the one that's real?

If your current version of success feels like performance, it's okay to pause. It's okay to question. It's okay to evolve. You are not failing—you're awakening.

You get to redefine success as many times as you need. You're allowed to outgrow old dreams. You're allowed to want less of what the world says you should want—and more of what brings you alive.

And maybe—just maybe—success isn't something to strive for. Maybe it's something to remember. Something that's already within you. A life that feels good, not just looks good.

## A New Success Story

It's okay if your definition of success changes. It should.

You are not static. Your soul is not meant to stay the same.

As you heal, grow, and realign, your values shift. Your desires deepen. Your priorities become clearer. That's not confusion—that's wisdom. That's evolution.

So here's your invitation:
- Redefine what success means for you.
- Let go of metrics that don't reflect your heart.
- Choose a version of winning that feels soulful.

Let it include:

- Rest
- Love
- Laughter
- Freedom
- Truth
- Fulfillment
- A morning you don't dread
- A body you feel safe in
- A purpose that energizes you
- Relationships that nourish your spirit

Because that's not just success. That's a life well lived.

That's a life aligned.

And that? That's the kind of winning that truly matters.

## A Reflection Practice

Take a few quiet moments and journal your answers to these:

- What does success feel like—not look like—for me?
- Where in my life am I chasing someone else's definition of success?
- What am I ready to release?
- What am I ready to reclaim?

Let these reflections guide your next steps. Let them anchor your truth.

You don't need to earn your worth through productivity. You don't need to prove your value through performance.

You are already enough. Right here. Right now.

And the most successful thing you can do? Is to live from that truth.

# Chapter 20:

# Integration—Embodying Your Evolution

---

*"The longest journey you will ever take is the one from your head to your heart."*
— **Sioux Proverb**

Awareness is the beginning. Insight opens the door. But it's integration that invites lasting change. It's one thing to know what needs to shift—it's another to embody that knowing in your everyday life.

This is the chapter where healing becomes habit. Where lessons become lived. Where your evolution becomes embodied.

Integration isn't loud. It's not flashy. It doesn't always come with fanfare. But it's potent. It's the quiet revolution that changes everything.

## From Knowing to Living

You've read the words. Reflected on the pages. Maybe even cried, laughed, or journaled along the way. You've uncovered truths. Named what no longer fits. Remembered who you are.

Now, the invitation is simple: live it.

- Don't just believe you're worthy—act like it.
- Don't just know your boundaries—honor them.
- Don't just talk about slowing down—practice it.

Integration is when your life begins to mirror your healing. When your actions reflect your awareness. When your truth moves from your head... into your heart... and all the way into your body.

## What Integration Looks Like

It's subtle but profound. You'll know you're integrating when:

- You pause and breathe before reacting.
- You notice an old trigger—and choose a new response.
- You speak kindly to yourself after a mistake.
- You walk away from what no longer serves, without guilt.
- You rest—not as a reward, but as a right.
- You make choices that feel aligned, not just expected.

It's not about perfection. It's about consistency, compassion, and courage.

## Let the Body Catch Up

Change isn't just cognitive—it's somatic. Your nervous system needs time to catch up with your mindset. Be patient with the process.

Let rest be sacred. Let rituals be your anchors. Let your body become a trusted ally in your healing. Movement, breathwork, meditation, dance, stillness—these are the languages of integration.

When you practice presence in the body, your healing becomes more than an idea. It becomes lived wisdom.

## A Life That Reflects the Work

Integration shows up in the choices you make when no one's watching:

- The boundaries you now set without apology.
- The relationships that feel reciprocal, not draining.
- The joy you no longer feel guilty for embracing.
- The peace that comes from not needing to prove anything anymore.

It's the quiet confidence of someone who has come home to themselves.

## From the Page to Your Path

This chapter is an invitation to take everything you've learned and make it real:

- Create a morning ritual that grounds you.
- Journal your truth before making decisions.
- Set small intentions for how you want to feel each day.
- Return to your breath, again and again.

These simple acts are how you integrate a new way of being. Integration isn't something you check off a list. It's something you return to—daily, gently, lovingly.

## You Are Not Who You Were

And that's the point. You've softened, strengthened, unraveled, and reclaimed. You've cracked open and realigned.

You've remembered parts of yourself you forgot. You've released roles you no longer want to play. You've written new definitions of worth, success, love, and healing.

Now it's time to live them. Embody them. Be them.

## Welcome to Your Integration

This isn't an ending. It's a continuation. A return. A rebirth.

You don't need to chase the next breakthrough. You just need to embody what you already know.

Let alignment guide your steps. Let embodiment become your daily devotion.

And let your life—the way you show up, speak, rest, love, and lead—be the ultimate expression of your healing.

This is your integration. This is your arrival.

# Epilogue:
# The Journey Continues

---

*"You do not just wake up and become the butterfly. Growth is a process."*
**— Rupi Kaur**

You've walked through these pages with courage, curiosity, and heart. You've reflected. Released. Reclaimed. You've sat with discomfort, danced with truth, and dared to envision a life more aligned with who you really are.

And now?

Now you stand at a new threshold—not with all the answers, but with something even more powerful:

- A deeper knowledge of yourself
- A clearer sense of what matters
- A felt remembrance of your inner strength, your softness your soul

This isn't the end.

This is a beginning.

The unfolding.

The continuation of a journey only you can walk.

# This Book Was Never About Fixing You

You were never broken.

You were becoming.

Always becoming.

This book wasn't a manual—it was a mirror.

It was never about teaching you something new.

It was about **helping you remember what you already know.**

And now that you've remembered, it's time to **live it.**

# Your Integration in Real Time

Here's the invitation moving forward:

- Let your life reflect your healing.
- Let your days be grounded in truth, not performance.
- Let your relationships mirror your self-respect.
- Let your choices honor your evolution.

This isn't about being perfect. It's about being real.

Showing up honestly.

Choosing what aligns, again and again.

Even when it's hard.

Especially when it's hard.

# Keep Returning to Yourself

- When you feel lost—come back to your breath.
- When you feel overwhelmed—simplify.
- When you doubt—reconnect with your why.
- When you forget how far you've come—reread the words that once reminded you.

Let this book be your companion—not a one-time read, but a lifelong reference.

- A touchstone for your truth.
- A gentle nudge back to center.

# This Is the Work. This Is the Gift.

**The healing**

**The becoming**

**The daily practice of alignment, of softness, of strength.**

- You are the work of an artist
- You are the unfolding and the observer.
- You are the storm and the stillness.
- You are your own greatest guide.

You have everything you need inside of you.

- Your wisdom.
- Your wildness.
- Your worth.

So keep choosing you.

# What Comes Next

- Keep walking your path—with heart, integrity, and fierce devotion to your growth.
- Keep rewriting the story when it no longer fits.
- Keep showing up—with grace, with fire, with unshakable softness.

**Your story is still unfolding**

**Your light is still rising**

**Your truth is still deepening**

And if you'd like a companion for that journey—a space to continue integrating, reflecting, and realigning—I've created **The Built Stronger Journal: A Soulful Companion to Your Transformation** just for you.

» Use it to explore your truths more deeply.

» Let it hold your intentions, your questions, your daily wisdom.

» Return to it when you need grounding, inspiration, or a loving nudge forward.

You don't need all the answers—just the courage to keep listening.

And I, for one, can't wait to see what you create with it.

# Final Words

Built stronger.

Not in spite of the journey, but because of it.

From the inside out—and always with love.

Warmly,

**Bonnie Strati**

Be Soulful Coaching

www.ingramcontent.com/pod-product-compliance
Lightning Source LLC
Chambersburg PA
CBHW070548090426
42735CB00013B/3103